Original title:
Puns Beneath the Pines

Copyright © 2025 Creative Arts Management OÜ
All rights reserved.

Author: Rafael Sterling
ISBN HARDBACK: 978-1-80567-392-7
ISBN PAPERBACK: 978-1-80567-691-1

Riddles amongst the Roots

In the shade where shadows play,
Laughter skips and finds its way.
Mossy jokes on branches swing,
Nature holds the comic ring.

Knotted tales in leafy words,
Whispers soft among the birds.
Roots entangle in wit and jest,
Beneath the boughs, we're truly blessed.

Jolly Remarks in the Thicket

Through the brambles, giggles bloom,
Echoes chase away the gloom.
Breezy quips float in the air,
Jolly tales spun without a care.

Squirrels share their nutty jokes,
Trees chuckle, playing folks.
In this thicket, smiles conspire,
Hearts ignite in warm desire.

Frolics Under the Foliate

Leaves are dancing, voices rise,
Jesting all beneath the skies.
Acorns drop with little thuds,
Tickling toes in earthy muds.

Frolics spark with every glance,
Nature's own comical dance.
Underneath the verdant maze,
Laughter lingers, joy ablaze.

Sly Smiles in Nature's Embrace

Amidst the branches, secrets twine,
Whimsical whispers, oh how divine!
Little critters with sly, sweet grins,
Chase each other, laughter spins.

Beneath the boughs, a playful game,
Nature's wit, it warms the same.
In this embrace, both sly and bright,
Joyful moments take their flight.

Lighthearted Moments Under the Limbs

In the shade where the branches sway,
A squirrel jokes about his day.
He's nuts, you see, in every way,
Chasing acorns, come what may.

The breeze whispers tales of old,
Of oak trees, wise and bold.
The pine trees giggle, breaking the mold,
While capturing laughter like stories told.

A woodpecker knocks, a rhythmic beat,
Telling secrets where shadows meet.
With a chirp, he says, 'Life's a treat!'
Under the limbs, let fun repeat.

Sunshine dapples, laughter rings,
Every rustle, a song that sings.
Nature's stage where joy springs,
In this space, happiness clings.

Jocular Journeys through the Timber

On a trail where the tall trees bend,
Every path seems to twist and lend.
A rabbit asks, 'Where did you send
Those carrots? I can't comprehend!'

The deer quips, 'Just down the lane,
But now I think I'm going insane.
With all this chatter, it's such a strain,
Can't a fellow just eat in vain?'

Each rustling leaf has a tale to weave,
Of friendship formed and tricks up their sleeve.
A family of raccoons gives a reprieve,
Sharing jokes that make you believe.

As shadows stretch and daylight fades,
Laughter echoes through nature's glades.
With every step, delight cascades,
In these woods, joy never evades.

Sarcasm in the Swaying Spruce

In the woods where the tall trees sway,
A spruce chuckles, 'What's new today?'
'Oh, just the usual, come what may,
Same old jokes that we replay.'

Anowl hoots, 'You think you're wise?
I'm tired of your silly lies!'
With every snicker, tension flies,
Amusement dances under the skies.

A fox joins in with a sly grin,
'What's a timber without a spin?
Lay down your roots and join the din,
Let's have some laughs and all win.'

With whispers of wit among the leaves,
The forest teems with playful thieves.
A world of humor, nothing achieves,
Such joy as nature's trickster weaves.

Clever Conversations in the Clearing

In a clearing where the sun spills bright,
Friendship blooms in pure delight.
A chipmunk boasts of his last flight,
'It took skill, not just sheer might!'

The badger chuckles, 'You're quite the star,
But flying high is not your bar.
A digger's life won't get you far,
Stick to the ground and raise the jar!'

With splashes of laughter and playful glee,
Each creature chatters under the tree.
Their jokes ring out like bumblebees,
Pollinating smiles, wild and free.

As evening falls and shadows blend,
The forest friends know laughter's trend.
With clever talk, the fun won't end,
In the clearing, joy will extend.

Whispers of Woody Wordplay

In the shade of green, jokes sprout wide,
A tree-mendous laugh, come take a ride.
Roots of humor, twisted and wild,
Nature's own jest, like a playful child.

Branches bend low, cradling cheer,
With every rustle, fun draws near.
Falling acorns, riddles in disguise,
Under bark jokes, wisdom's surprise.

Amidst the leaves, giggles do twine,
Squirrels joke softly, in woodland line.
With each playful breeze, puns take flight,
In this forest of fun, all feels right.

So gather 'round, let laughter conspire,
With each wooden quip, hearts lift higher.
In every creak, a chuckle will find,
Whispers of humor, so perfectly aligned.

Jests in the Canopy

High up above, the branches weave,
A tapestry of jokes we believe.
Knots of giggles, round every turn,
Amusing fables for all who yearn.

Leaves are laughing, swaying in time,
Nature's humor, so sweet and prime.
The owls at night, wisecrackers of lore,
Sharing their wisdom, while we want more.

Rabbits hop in with puns in their pocket,
A fox's sly grin, a woodland docket.
Every rustling fern, a tickle, a tease,
In this lighthearted grove, laughs do appease.

So sit with me, under the leafy dome,
Where giggles and snickers are always at home.
In the canopy's arms, find joy in the sights,
For here love and laughter dance through the nights.

Timbered Tales of Wit

Amongst the logs and shady expanse,
Lies a tale of laughter, come join the dance.
The trees lean close, eager to share,
Their whispered wisdom, light as air.

Stumps spin stories, tall as the sky,
A sapling's spunk, the limit's the high.
Bark can sometimes be a literal jest,
For those with a punchline, life is a fest.

With mushrooms sprouting their own little jokes,
The squirrels chatter like lively folks.
In every ring, a tale unfolds,
Of playful hearts and spirits bold.

So gather 'round, friends both young and old,
To timbered theatrics, let's be sold.
For life is a stage, and this is the show,
In the forest of laughter, we all will grow.

Laughter Among the Branches

Beneath the tall trees, laughter resounds,
Joking with leaves, where joy abounds.
A family of sparrows, chirps filled with glee,
In this merry grove, we are wild and free.

Acorns knock-knock, the jokes start to flow,
While pinecones giggle, putting on a show.
Each fluttering leaf, a comedic race,
A woodsy carnival, a funny place.

Dancing in shadows, we let laughter play,
As fireflies twinkle, and night turns to day.
In every whisper, fun hangs around,
While nature sings softly, a curious sound.

So come join the laughter, let worries fall,
With each tree's punchline, we'll give it our all.
In this realm of mirth, nothing feels quite right,
Like laughter among branches, a pure delight.

Lighthearted Laughs in Leafy Retreats

In the shade, the squirrels chip,
As acorns roll, they start to flip.
A crow caws loud, oh what a tease,
As branches sway with playful ease.

A picnic spread, a sandwich stacked,
But ants march forth, they're well-packed.
With each small bite, there's a new game,
Who knew a meal could bring such fame?

The breeze brings whispers, leaves that sway,
A joke about a tree—who'll hear it play?
Giggles bounce with every word,
In laughter's arms, we're all assured.

Under stars, the fireflies glow,
They dance around, putting on a show.
A punchline here, a pun or two,
In leafy retreats, all joy ensues.

Amusing Anecdotes from the Arbor

The trunks stand tall, but tales are short,
Of lumberjack dreams and forest sport.
Branches bend with a chuckle bright,
As squirrels trade puns, a happy sight.

Leaves gossip softly, secrets they share,
With every rustle, humor fills the air.
A woodpecker knocks, a beat so fine,
With rhythm like this, how can we pine?

Among the roots, a tortoise grins,
While rabbits laugh at their silly spins.
They hop and trot, with winks and cheer,
Creating joy while we wander near.

At twilight's hush, a whisper shared,
A tale of trees that truly dared.
With every chuckle, our hearts ignite,
In the shade of the boughs, laughter feels right.

Zany Zest Under the Cedars

Beneath the Cedars, the scene's a blast,
Where shadows play and moments last.
A lizard struts in shades of green,
With witty quips that make us beam.

The forest floor is a stage for fun,
Where each small creature's on the run.
A raccoon jests with a crafty gaze,
Stealing hearts in mischievous ways.

The breezes carry a tingle of cheers,
As laughter flies and dances near.
A funky tune from crickets' bands,
Inviting all to clap their hands.

The cedar trees sway, they lend their cheer,
In zany zest, we all draw near.
With twists and turns of every line,
We celebrate life, so sweet and fine.

Quirky Quests through the Pines

Through the pines, we wander wide,
With quirky quests and friends beside.
A toad croaks jokes from mossy stones,
While pinecones chuckle in muffled tones.

A trail of humor, we follow well,
Where every twist holds a silly spell.
A fox with flair and clever tricks,
Makes each step feel like a fix.

With shadows stretching as day departs,
We share our dreams, our laughs, our arts.
A night of wonder beneath the stars,
Where quirky quests bring no old scars.

In laughter's glow, we find our way,
Through pines and friends, in pure ballet.
Each moment shared, a story spun,
In quirky quests, we've only begun.

Capers in the Canopy

In branches high, a squirrel's dance,
He juggles acorns, takes a chance.
A robin chirps a punny song,
While shadows stretch the whole day long.

With laughter echoing from above,
The tree trunks whisper tales of love.
A raccoon wearing shades so cool,
Teaches the others the wise old rule.

Koalas munch on leaves with grace,
Cracking jokes in the leafy space.
They hang around, not missing a beat,
In this leafy realm, life is sweet.

So when you stroll beneath the green,
Join the mirth, embrace the scene.
For in the shade, where giggles flow,
Nature's humor steals the show.

Delights from the Dusty Trails

Footsteps crunch on the winding path,
Where laughter echoes, sparking its wrath.
A turtle jokes of racing speed,
While sprightly squirrels plant their seed.

Beneath the sky, with clouds like cream,
A piglet squeals, "I love to dream!"
As daisies wink and wildflowers giggle,
Violets blush and frogs all wiggle.

Each twist and turn, a playful jest,
Laughter lingers, it's simply the best.
A fox quips, "Why did the hen cross?
To get to the joke, or be the boss!"

So wander wide, let joy prevail,
Discover life on every trail.
Among the dust, where fun prevails,
Find whimsical wonders in joyous tales.

Glee beneath the Glade

In a shady nook, the critters meet,
Frogs croak jokes, oh what a treat!
A chipmunk yells, "I've got a plan!
Let's prank the owl, if we can!"

A gentle breeze spins leaves around,
The laughter rises from the ground.
A hedgehog spins a yarn so tight,
Everyone chuckles at the sight.

The mushrooms sway, all painted bright,
Two snails race by, speedy as light.
Amid the trees, where fun is laid,
There's glee galore, and laughter played.

So gather close, the sun's on high,
Join in the tunes, let spirits fly.
For beneath the glade, in every shade,
Life's humorous tales are serenely made.

The Humor of Hidden Hollows

In hidden nooks, where shadows creep,
A badger tells jokes that make you leap.
With flicks of tails and gentle grins,
The whole wood laughs, where fun begins.

A wise old owl with glasses round,
Shares puns that echo from tree to ground.
"Why do trees never get lost?"
"Because they know all paths at no cost!"

Branches sway, a rhythm divine,
As laughter blends with a sweet sunshine.
A curious fox tilts his head,
"Who's been sleeping in my flowerbed?"

So venture deep where secrets lie,
And humor sings in the soft blue sky.
In hidden hollows, let the laughter blaze,
For life is best in the funniest ways.

Cheery Chatter beneath the Canopy

Beneath a tree of endless cheer,
Squirrels gossip, far and near.
With acorns tossed like jokes in flight,
They giggle softly, day and night.

A branch swings low, a wink begins,
Crickets chirp their verdant spins.
The leaves all laugh, in rustling flow,
Tickling the sky, they steal the show.

When shadows stretch and brighten the glade,
The chatter turns to a freshly-made trade.
With vows to share a nutty delight,
They find delight in silly sight.

So here we'll gather, what a blast!
A ticklish tale from the leafy past.
The canopy laughs in colors so bright,
Where every chuckle shines in light.

Jesting Journeys of the Whispering Woods

Through winding paths, where whispers play,
The trees have secrets, come what may.
With every step, a joke appears,
That tickles softly, dries the tears.

A bear in boots, a cap on tight,
Dances in circles, oh, what a sight!
Raccoons with hats, prance on by,
Swapping high fives while fluttering by.

Boughs sway gently, telling tales,
Of pirate squirrels and cheeky snails.
The woods echo with laughter's embrace,
As woodland creatures find their space.

So join the fun, take a stroll,
A pun-filled journey, heart and soul.
Amidst the pines where giggles reside,
Adventure awaits, come take a ride.

Joyous Sojourns through the Sylvan

In golden glades where laughter springs,
The sun sets low, and nature sings.
A fox tells tales of moonlit fun,
While rabbits hop, two by one.

Every flower wearing a quirky grin,
Winks at visitors drawn from within.
The daisies talk, the violets laugh,
As nature crafts a clever path.

With pinecone hats and leafy shields,
The woodland critters dance in fields.
A chorus of smiles fills the air,
As every critter has a share.

So in this grove of smiles and cheer,
Join the jesters, shed your fear.
For life is bright and laughter sweet,
In joyous journeys, we find our beat.

Laughs Layered in Lushness

In shadowed corners, whispers grow,
The forest echoes, a comedic show.
With every rustle, a giggle's tossed,
In layers of green, no laugh is lost.

Frogs in tuxes leap with glee,
While bees wear crowns, sipping tea.
A dapper deer prances with flair,
Making merry with woodland air.

The ferns sway soft, a dance of fun,
As every creature joins the run.
With peals of laughter, roots entwined,
The joy of nature, perfectly aligned.

So find your place beneath this bough,
Let nature's humor take a bow.
For in this paradise, we unite,
With laughter layered, pure delight.

Barking Up the Right Tree

In the woods where whispers sway,
Trees tell tales in a playful way.
Roots twist like jokes on a sunny morn,
Branches bob like laughter reborn.

Squirrels scamper with a nutty grin,
Cracking jokes as they scurry in.
Each leaf flutters with a wink and nod,
Nature's jesters, a joyful facade.

Coniferous Chuckles

Pine cones tumble like playful rhymes,
Tickling the ground in merry chimes.
The needles giggle, rustling light,
Cracking up under the moon's bright sight.

Fir trees sway like jolly jesters,
Bouncing humor with woodland festers.
The air is thick with giggles galore,
Echoing laughter that begs for more.

Nature's Tongue-in-Cheek

Whispers drift from bark to breeze,
Clever quips that aim to please.
The rustling leaves, a cheeky tease,
Nature's humor flows with ease.

Critters conspire in playful glee,
Rabbits and foxes share their spree.
A clever badger makes a pun,
Under shadows, the laughter's spun.

Leafy Laughter

Leaves chuckle as the wind draws near,
Tickling branches, spreading cheer.
Each gust carries a joke anew,
A symphony of giggles in the dew.

Mossy cushions cradle wit so soft,
Where shadows dance and spirits loft.
Every trunk and twig a prankster's game,
In this woodland where laughter is name.

Loquacious Lore

The trees conspire with tales to tell,
Whispering secrets that charm so well.
Underneath the canopy's embrace,
Every branch holds a comic place.

A woodpecker drums like a stand-up king,
Filling the air with a punchy zing.
Nature spins tales that tickle the soul,
In this forest, laughter is the goal.

Gags among the Greenery

Under branches wide and bright,
Laughter blooms like flowers white.
The squirrel jokes with a sunny twitch,
While the thistle blushes, just a glitch.

With each critter's pun-filled chime,
Nature laughs, a merry rhyme.
The pine tree leans, it can't contain,
A joke that echoes in the rain.

Frogs croak jokes with ribbit cheer,
While bees buzz puns as friends draw near.
The forest floor is rich with glee,
In this wild comedy spree!

Mirthful Encounters in the Evergreen

Among the needles sharp and keen,
A bumblebee winks, looking serene.
"Buzz off!" it says with a playful grin,
While the fox chuckles, taking it in.

A pair of raccoons trade sly replies,
As sunlight dances in the skies.
They share secrets beneath the oak,
Where laughter flows like a gentle poke.

The partridge struts, a showy display,
Cracking wise with a feathery sway.
Each branch vibrates with fun-filled flair,
In this haven of humor, none can compare.

The Art of Wit in the Wilderness

In a glade where jokes take flight,
The chipmunks gather, a quirky sight.
With nutty puns they toss around,
While owls hoot wisdom profound.

The tall pine whispers a sweet tease,
As the raccoons giggle, swaying with ease.
Creekside, a turtle cracks a grin,
Saying, "Slow down, it's where we begin!"

Count the leaves, they tell you true,
Nature's jokes are evergreen too.
With every breeze, the laughter wafts,
Into the wild, where joy never drafts.

Satirical Strolls on the Trail

On a winding path of leafy dreams,
The humor springs, or so it seems.
A moose quips, "My antlers are neat,
But these shoes? They're just a treat!"

The hikers snicker at deer's wisecracks,
As they hike up nature's tracks.
"Watch out for roots," they all recite,
"The trip is fun, but won't be light!"

With whispers of whimsy in the breeze,
The forest joins in, aims to please.
A playful romp, a witty spree,
In every corner, jesters are free!

Lively Laughter in the Leafscape

In the grove where shadows dance,
Jokes take flight, given a chance.
Trees chuckle as branches sway,
Whispering secrets of their play.

Under leaves, we break the mold,
Tales of squirrels, cheeky and bold.
Nature's jesters, so spry and spry,
Chasing clouds that drift on high.

Beneath the boughs, we find delight,
Each bark a pun, each bark so light.
Mirth flows freely, a joyful stream,
Happy hearts in the leafy dream.

As sunlight glimmers, the humor grows,
Laughter echoes where the wild wind blows.
With every chuckle, we're forever entwined,
In a forest rich with threads of the mind.

Snickers in the Sundrenched Pines

Where sunlight filters through green trails,
Giggles rise with the softest gales.
Among the trunks, whimsy takes flight,
Turning the day into pure delight.

The critters gather, sharing their wit,
Bouncing banter, never a split.
From pinecone tales to acorn jests,
Their merry mischief gives nature its zest.

In the warm glow of the glowing dawn,
Laughter weaves like a playful fawn.
Silly shadows on the forest floor,
Invite us in for just a bit more.

With every breeze, chuckles return,
In this haven where smiles brightly burn.
Sun-drenched pines hold secrets of cheer,
Whispered in smiles both far and near.

Banter on the Boughs

Up high in the trees, the gossip flows,
Chattering leaves, where humor grows.
Branches sway with playful charm,
Creating a stage, no need for alarm.

With owl-like wisdom, the wise one hoots,
Sharing punchlines and silly roots.
While squirrels crack jokes with a twitch of the tail,
Their antics weaving a whimsical trail.

In the boughs where the bluebirds sing,
Laughter is crafted on nature's wing.
Each note carries joy through the mist,
Unexpected humor you won't want to miss.

As twilight glimmers, and shadows near,
Banter and giggles float all year.
Nature's comedians, full of grace,
Find happiness in this leafy place.

Twists of Wit in the Thicket

In the thicket where the wild things laugh,
Every twig spins a humorous craft.
With every rustle, a quip appears,
Creating a symphony of light-hearted cheers.

Beneath the brambles, the jokes take root,
Nature's punchlines, oh so astute.
Bouncing back with a giggling spree,
The thicket's a haven for jokes and glee.

A rabbit hops by with a cheeky grin,
Playfully tossing a line to begin.
While the trees shake off their leafy chaff,
Each twist of wit generates a hearty laugh.

As dusk drapes softly, the laughter stays,
Carving out joy in a million ways.
In this thicket, cleverness grows,
A joyful tapestry life truly shows.

Evergreen Etymology

The trees stand tall, roots so deep,
Whispering secrets that they keep.
A conifer's tale, oh what a lark,
Beneath their branches, we spark a quark.

With needles sharp, they take a jab,
'Wood' you believe, they're quite the fab?
From pine nuts to jokes, it's quite the grind,
Nature's humor is for us to find.

Come join the fun, let's play around,
With every branch, laughter is found.
Ode to the bark, the leaves that sway,
A giggle, a chuckle, let's laugh away!

So gather close, hear the tree's own jest,
In the shade of green, we are truly blessed.

Quips from the Forest Floor

Underneath the canopy so wide,
Lies a world of jests that cannot hide.
From acorns cracking with a snappy flare,
To squirrels who dance without a care.

The forest floor, a stage of fun,
Where every leaf shines like the sun.
Roots twist and turn in playful ways,
Inviting all to join the fray.

Mushrooms chuckle beneath the shade,
In soft-spoken tones, they serenade.
With every shadow, a pun is born,
In the laughter of trees, we are reborn.

So let's take a stroll, just you and I,
Among the giggles that flutter high.

Pine-Scented Puns

In the boughs up high, where laughter drips,
Fables flow like sap from leafy tips.
Each whisper carries a scented jest,
As laughter lingers, feeling so blessed.

With pine so fresh, it tickles the air,
Jokes spread like needles, everywhere.
Branches sway with a knowing grin,
It's all in good fun beneath the skin.

So grab a seat 'neath the fragrant trees,
And enjoy the banter with care-free ease.
Nature cooks up a humorous roast,
Among the greens, we'll raise a toast!

For every swing, there's a giggle or two,
In the cozy shade, come join the crew!

Spruce and Semantics

Spruce up the mood with words so bright,
In the forest's embrace, laughter takes flight.
From timber puns to leafy lore,
Vegetative wit, we'll always explore.

Branching out with every quip,
Nature composes a playful script.
Leaves fluttering with giggles resound,
As the trees share what's been found.

In every crack and crinkle of bark,
Lives a wordplay that hits the mark.
So gather 'round for a pun-filled spree,
Where nature and humor craft harmony.

In this thicket of wit, we'll thrive,
With every chuckle, we come alive.

Laughter in the Leafy Lanes

In leafy lanes where laughter sways,
The trees wear smiles on sunny days.
Acorns drop with a playful thud,
While squirrels plot their nutty flood.

With branches reaching, tickling air,
A breeze brings giggles everywhere.
Mushrooms sprout in silly forms,
Whispering jokes in mushroom storms.

The path winds on with glee and cheer,
As critters dance, their friends all near.
Nature's jesters, wild and free,
Making merry, just wait and see!

So come along, enjoy the ride,
Through laughter's lane, let joy abide.
For every twist, a punchline waits,
Amidst the trees, we've found our mates.

Jestful Shadows of the Forest

In forest deep where shadows play,
The sunlight beams in a quirky way.
Trees tell tales with creaky voice,
In nature's joke, we all rejoice.

A fox in shades of red and gold,
Tells secrets whispered, stories bold.
Branches sway with a gentle tease,
As leaves do dance upon the breeze.

Moss-covered stones, a throne of fun,
Where laughter rings from everyone.
The wise old owl, with wit so sly,
Keeps watch for jesters flying by.

So wander forth with hearts so light,
Through jestful shadows, pure delight.
In every nook, a smile you'll find,
As laughter echoes, warm and kind.

Playful Pines and Snappy Lines

Among the pines where laughter sings,
The breeze hums low, and joy takes wing.
Pinecones tumble, a comical sight,
As nature's punchlines take to flight.

A squirrel leaps with acrobatic flair,
Diving from branches, without a care.
"Catch me if you can!" he seems to say,
In playful banter of the day.

The sun breaks through with a beaming grin,
Warming the world, inviting in.
Each shadow plays its silly game,
While laughter echoes, still the same.

So join the fun, lose all your strife,
In playful pines, enjoy your life.
For every chuckle shared in glee,
Unites us all, you and me!

Banter Among the Branches

In branches high where whispers flow,
The trees hold secrets we long to know.
Their leaves share jests with rustling sighs,
While critters chuckle 'neath sunny skies.

A chipmunk grins, his cheeks quite full,
Stashing snacks, he's never dull.
With every nibble, there's a pun,
"From the pantry to the fun, I run!"

A breeze sweeps in, a soft caress,
Each branch and twig, in joyful dress.
With every snap and crackling sound,
Banter flourishes all around.

So take a pause, embrace the scene,
Let laughter linger, bright and keen.
For in this grove, where fun combines,
We find our joy, in jokes and signs.

Snappy Sagas in the Pines

In the woods where squirrels play,
Trees gossip about their day,
One tall pine thinks it's so neat,
That ants march to its leafy beat.

With branches stretched to tell a tale,
A rabbit laughed, but often failed,
For every joke came with a hitch,
That joke-telling tree was quite the witch.

So when the sun sets, and stars align,
All creatures gather, it's simply divine,
Under that tree, laughter does climb,
Life in the pines is truly sublime!

Yet one night, a wise owl took flight,
Challenging the pine to a pun-filled fight,
And as the night wore on, oh what a sight,
Even the moon chuckled with pure delight!

Jovial Journeys of the Junipers

By the creek where junipers sway,
A hedgehog tried to change his way,
He tumbled 'round, in floral spree,
Saying, "Can someone just roll with me?"

The wise old juniper gave a grin,
"You're quirky! Let the fun begin!"
With each twist, humor took flight,
As they danced under the moonlight.

From that day on, they roamed so far,
Junipers and hedgehogs, the best of stars,
Through laughter shared, their joy was known,
In silly moments, true love had grown.

So if you wander where shadows align,
You might just see them in the pine,
With every giggle, their hearts entwine,
Creating memories, oh so fine!

Fickle Fables of the Forest

In the forest, where whispers weave,
A fox once donned a magician's sleeve,
"Watch me turn this leaf into gold!"
But it flipped and flopped, quite uncontrolled.

Said the owl, perched high on a limb,
"That was a trick, rather dim!"
The fox, undeterred, made another plan,
"I'll show you magic, so just a span!"

A squirrel rolled in nuts galore,
Cried out, "This feast is never a bore!"
Yet each attempt to impress the crowd,
Had laughter echoing, happy and loud.

So under branches where stories twist,
Fables unfold with a sprinkle of mist,
In this quirky world, they cheer and jest,
Finding humor is always the best!

Folly in the Foliage

Deep in the leaves where the sun plays,
A turtle tried to join the ballet,
With twirls and spins, oh what a sight,
But fell flat—still a glorious night!

The butterflies giggled, high in the air,
Spreading rumors with delicate flair,
"Do you see that show? It's one to thrill!"
Each drift of the breeze carried their will.

A wise old tree, with bark so grand,
Said, "Laughter's the music, take a stand!"
So they danced together, sometimes in sync,
Creating a melody to spark and to wink.

With folly wrapped in each bright branch,
The foliage hummed as if in a dance,
In nature's embrace, fun filled the air,
A whimsical tale, beyond compare!

Echoes of Enigmatic Etymology

In the woods, words play hide and seek,
Where roots of language twist and creak.
The trees giggle as they sway and bend,
Whispering secrets only they comprehend.

A squirrel named Nutty tells a tale,
Of acorns that danced without fail.
His rhymes bring laughter, such a sight,
As leafy laughter fills the night.

Branches chuckle, their leaves in a whirl,
As vines weave stories, a wonderful swirl.
Each bark tells of old tales anew,
While shadows of wordplay mingle too.

With each step, a joke on the breeze,
Nature's humor, sure to please.
Amongst the pines, wisdom we find,
Echoes of etymology, one of a kind.

Pinecone Punchlines

Gather 'round for the chuckles to bloom,
Where laughter and pinecones fill the room.
Each caper shared like nutty delight,
Jokes floating high, taking flight.

A pinecone declared, "I'm nature's best seed!"
While others just laughed at the hearty deed.
"I'm pine-solutely perfect," one teased with glee,
As branches laughed, swinging free.

Laughter echoed through foresty halls,
As critters delighted in punchlines and calls.
Each tickle of humor, a woodland surprise,
With chuckling accents that rise to the skies.

So join in the fun, let the quips unwind,
Pinecone punchlines, the best of their kind.
In this forest of giggles, let's dance and prance,
Where humor is hearty and free to enhance.

Savoring Shenanigans in the Sunlight

Sunlight spills gold on the soft forest floor,
Where mischief unfolds, and laughter can soar.
A rabbit named Chuck hops with flair,
Daring squirrels to join in the dare.

"Why did the tree break up?" he said with a wink,
"Because it couldn't find the right type to link!"
The sunlit stage, a spectacle bright,
Where jokes share the warmth in the soft twilight.

In shady spots, where shadows play,
The sunbeams dance in a silly ballet.
With laughter as syrup, so sweet and divine,
Savoring shenanigans under the pines.

So gather your friends, let the fun begin,
As laughter echoes, the trees give a grin.
In this glade of jests, take a moment to stay,
And relish the joy of a sunshiny day.

Canopies of Cleverness

Beneath the green canopies of clever wit,
Where bright ideas and puns all sit.
A crow caws out a riddle or two,
As giggles and snickers float on through.

"Oh, what a bark!" the wise owl would say,
"Laughter is free, so come out and play!"
Each branch bears witness to quips on the go,
Enticing the critters with strife and flow.

Beneath the tall pines, the jokes intertwine,
As shadows cast laughter, both silly and fine.
Breezy remarks drift like leaves in a dance,
In the canopies' charm, we twirl and prance.

So revel in riddles that float with the breeze,
In this forest of fun, our spirits we tease.
With each little chuckle, the world feels anew,
A canopy of cleverness, just waiting for you.

Rustic Revelations

In a glade where laughter grows,
The trees chuckle with their prose.
Squirrels dance, with jokes so spry,
They tickle the branches, oh my oh my!

Mushrooms pop with tiny grins,
As whispers spread like breezy winds.
The brook babbles tales of cheer,
Bringing smiles both far and near.

A raccoon tells of stolen pies,
While owl winks with knowing eyes.
Each twig and leaf, a punchline neat,
Nature's humor, oh so sweet!

Underneath the starlit dome,
The woods come alive, a jovial home.
With every rustle, a playful tease,
The forest echoes with delightful ease.

Whispers of the Witty Woods

In the woods, where shadows play,
The trees engage in witty fray.
A squirrel mocks the drowsy deer,
While breezes carry giggles here.

Branches stretch, they crack a joke,
As leaves flutter and softly poke.
Mossy beds hold secrets tight,
Revealing puns in the moonlight.

Beneath the canopy, soft and wide,
Playful spirits choose to hide.
The laughter echoes, crisp and clear,
As shadows dance, we hold them dear.

Every rustle, a merry cheer,
In the woods where joy draws near.
With giggles shared, our hearts align,
In nature's laugh, we intertwine.

Jests on the Journey

Along the path where wildflowers bloom,
A traveler smiles, dispelling gloom.
With every step, a tale unfolds,
As nature's punchlines break the molds.

A chipmunk chirps with witty grace,
Casting shadows upon the place.
The brook teases with splashing sound,
Wit and whimsy all around.

Above, a crow caws in jest,
Challenging the sun to a light-hearted test.
Each pebble whispers, a laugh to share,
On this journey, we have a flair.

The hills echo with mirthful cries,
As butterflies share their comic ties.
In the woods, where giggles abound,
Every turn reveals joy profound.

Humor in the Hallowed Grove

In the hollowed woods, where spirits dwell,
The trees hold secrets they love to tell.
With branches waving a jovial cheer,
Even shadows can't help but disappear.

A fox prances, with tales so bright,
Of moonlit parties that last all night.
The owls chuckle with wise old eyes,
As twinkling stars join in the skies.

The mushrooms giggle, their caps a delight,
Sharing stories that spark the night.
With every rustle of leaf and vine,
Laughter echoes, sweet and fine.

In this grove of joy and jest,
Nature's laughter is truly blessed.
Here we gather, hearts ablaze,
In the humor of life, we dance and sway.

Rooted in Humor

In the shade where laughter grows,
Trees tell tales that no one knows.
Branches bend with humor's grace,
Filling hearts in this green space.

A squirrel stashed a nut or two,
He chuckled, saying, "Now, I'm through!"
With acorns rolling down the hill,
His jokes made everyone quite ill.

The woodpecker beats a funny drum,
A rhythm that makes all trees hum.
Tapping jokes, he's truly rare,
In the forest, laughter's in the air.

Beneath the boughs, the shadows play,
Tickling ribs at the end of the day.
Roots entwined in giggles deep,
In this grove, who dares to sleep?

Sappy Satire

Sap flows down from every tree,
Sticky stories, wild and free.
Maple sweetness, oh so bold,
A syrupy tale yet to be told.

The owls hoot a clever jest,
While hiding in their cozy nest.
With wisdom wrapped in every word,
Their irony can be absurd.

Bark of humor thick and rough,
Chasing the mundane never tough.
The pine cones play a game of puns,
A forest filled with giggling runs.

With whispers dancing through the leaves,
The tales of laughter interweaves.
In every nook and every dell,
The trees share secrets hard to quell.

Needles of Wit

Amidst the green, there's twisted fun,
Each needle sharp, a quip or pun.
Spruce with jokes, so fresh and bright,
A laughter fest from morn 'til night.

The chipmunk's grin, a cheeky spark,
He burrows deep—oh, what a lark!
Gathering lines, and jokes divine,
In the forest, wit will shine.

Branches sway to nature's beat,
While critters dance on tiny feet.
Laughter echoes through the trees,
A whimsical tune carried by the breeze.

Old trees chuckle with each sway,
Whispering stories of yesterday.
With needles poking at life's bliss,
Every moment wrapped in a twist.

Forest Frolics in Word Form

In the woods where whimsy thrives,
Nature's charm keeps laughter alive.
Beneath the canopy so wide,
Witty banter takes a ride.

The ferns fold up with gentle grace,
While spiders weave a silly face.
Their webs are puns in glistening strands,
Entangling trolls in funny jests and bands.

Logs roll over in a giggling spree,
Hilarity grows on every tree.
Mushrooms sprout with quirky glee,
A cap-on-cap of comedy!

And as the sun begins to set,
With all that laughter, never fret.
In this realm of wordy cheer,
The forest's heart beats loud and clear.

Arborous Antics

In the shade where whispers dwell,
Trees share secrets, tales to tell.
A bark so loud it shakes the ground,
As giggles echo all around.

Branches stretch like arms in play,
Leaves are laughing, come what may.
Roots entwine in silly dance,
Nature's jesters, take a chance!

Squirrels plot with acorn plots,
While frogs croak jokes and laugh a lot.
The grass ticks tickle tiny toes,
As sunlight winks beneath the bows.

Underneath a leafy dome,
Each tree presents a secret home.
Where laughter rings through knotted limbs,
And nature's humor never dims.

Grove of Gags

Among the trunks, a whisper spreads,
Where limbs twist jokes inside their heads.
A conifer jokes on a windy day,
While pine cones roll in a humorous way.

The creatures gather, all in line,
To share a jest or witty sign.
A beaver chuckles, 'What a sight!'
As the sun dips down, painting night.

Roots tangle up like storytellers,
Each grain of bark holds hidden fellers.
The owls wink knowingly from high,
As laughter leaps and fills the sky.

In this grove where jokes entwine,
A comedy show among the pine.
With quips and chuckles in the air,
This is the place for a playful dare.

Twisted Humor Trails

Take a stroll on the twisted path,
Where each step brings a hearty laugh.
Beneath the boughs, a pun takes flight,
And shadows giggle at the night.

Every turn a jest awaits,
With silly signs at all the gates.
A squirrel's tale or a rabbit's pun,
Trail of smiles, oh what fun!

The bark is rough, but jokes are smooth,
As trees and critters find their groove.
With every rustle, laughter swells,
Whispers curling like nature's spells.

Through these woods, the joy unfolds,
A story of humor, yet untold.
So step on through this merry maze,
And soak in all the funny rays.

Lumbering Laugh Lines

In a grove where giggles grow,
A lumberjack spins tales, you know.
With every chop, a chuckle rings,
As nature laughs at little things.

Logs stacked high like jokes on shelves,
Where trees remind us to be elves.
A knotted branch, a clumsy grin,
Nature's humor, let's dive in!

With each ring in the wood so fine,
Are stories built like perfect wine.
So raise a toast to funny trees,
Who sway and dance with playful breeze.

Beneath the bark, the laughter thrives,
As nature's humor springs alive.
In every move, in every line,
The joy of life, so sweet, divine.

Comedic Chatter under the Conifers

Beneath the branches, laughter rings,
A squirrel juggles acorns as it sings,
Trees whisper jokes in their leafy dress,
While nature giggles, causing quite a mess.

A pinecone hits, and it's a classic blunder,
Falling right on someone's head like thunder,
Echoes of chuckles, a chorus so merry,
Even the deer join in, don't you worry!

With needles sharp, they poke at our sides,
Mirthful moments, where playfulness hides,
Giggles bounce off every trunk and bough,
In the woods, it seems, we're all laughs somehow.

So gather round, where the tall trees sway,
With humor sprouting, let's shout hooray,
For under conifers, where the jokes align,
A tapestry of chuckles, all intertwined.

Jest in the Jungle of Pines

In a forest dense, where whispers conspire,
Trees play tricks that we all admire,
The wind tells tales, tickles like a breeze,
While shadows dance, bringing giggles with ease.

A banner of laughter unfurls on the trail,
As critters assemble, an amusing tale,
Squirrels hold court as their acorns align,
All sharing a jest, oh how they entwine!

Mushrooms in caps, costume party delight,
They sway to the rhythm, under moonlight,
Jokes take root in the soil so fine,
In this quaint jungle, all humor divine.

So roam through the pines, where jesters convene,
In the comedy undergrowth, surely unseen,
Each chuckle a branch, each giggle a vine,
In the jungle of pines, we laugh and we shine.

Smiles in the Shadows

In forests so deep, where secrets are small,
Smiles bloom bright like a festival ball,
With every turn, a grin takes its flight,
In shadows we gather, under pale moonlight.

The owls share wisdom, but wrapped in a grin,
They hoot of the antics the woodpeckers spin,
While rabbits exchange their mischievous tricks,
A tapestry woven with laughter and flicks.

The logs join the fun, a stage for the play,
As branches arch over, in humorous sway,
Each giggle ignited from beneath the bark,
Filling the night with a warm, joyful spark.

As whispers cascade, like a soft river flow,
We bask in the glow of this light-hearted show,
In shadows that dance, the woods echo smiles,
Where laughter will linger, for miles and miles.

Whimsy Woven into the Woods

In the heart of the forest, where whimsy is found,
Laughter weaves melodies, swirling around,
Branches sway gently, as if they can hear,
The tickles of joy that gather so near.

Each leaf a comedian, each twig a great jest,
Unruly and playful, they're all at their best,
With mushrooms as anchors in this wild bevy,
The woods come alive with laughter so heavy.

As squirrels recount their acorn adventures,
A chorus of giggles, sweet woodland dentures,
While shadows play tag in the dappled light,
In this tapestry woven, humor's delight.

So join in the laughter, let spirits unwind,
Embrace every chuckle that the forest has lined,
In whimsy's embrace, where joy has no bounds,
The woods are a stage, where hilarity resounds.

Chuckles in the Canopy

In branches where the laughter grows,
The squirrels tell the best of jokes.
A nutty punchline spills and flows,
While hickory stumps pull all the hoax.

Tall trees wear giggles like a cape,
Their leafy limbs in playful sway.
The owls hoot puns, no need to drape,
They wink at us, come join the fray.

The sunbeams tickle mossy beds,
As shadows dance and tease the light.
With every laugh, the world thread spreads,
A tapestry of pure delight.

So join the foliage's bright spree,
Where mirth wraps branches, thick and stout.
In this tall grove, so wild and free,
You'll find the fun is all about!

Quips in the Quiet Glade

Beneath the boughs where whispers dwell,
The critters exchange clever replies.
A feathered friend, with stories to sell,
Spins tales that make the time fly.

The brook chuckles, bubbling along,
As pebbles joke and giggle in play.
Each ripple sings a silly song,
While sunlight tickles the leaves' ballet.

Mushrooms wink, in polka dots dressed,
As rabbits hop with a jesting gait.
In every shadow, a smile's confessed,
In this glade, it's never too late.

So pause a moment, hear the cheer,
In nature's arms where joy does bloom.
With quips aplenty spreading near,
The quiet glade dispels all gloom!

Witty Wonders of the Woodland

In the heart of the woods, where humor's ripe,
The trees have tales that twist and turn.
Each trunk a stand-up, each branch a pipe,
From leafy lounges, wisdom to learn.

A witty fox crafts quips so sly,
With a flick of his tail, he steals the scene.
The rabbits chuckle as they hop by,
In this woodland play, all's merry and keen.

Bees buzz jokes while sipping sweet dew,
Their honeyed words are gold on the ground.
The sun's rays wrap the whole scene anew,
When laughter's the gift, and friendship's profound.

So meander through these sylvan halls,
Where wonders bloom with a punchline's finish.
In woodland's embrace, joy gently calls,
For in laughter's embrace, we all are replenished!

Wordplay in the Whispering Woods

In whispering woods, where secrets creep,
The trees hold jesters in their boughs.
Each rustle and chuckle, a gentle sweep,
Crafted in silence, as nature allows.

The ferns unfold, revealing their wit,
As crickets chirp puns with glee.
No need for a stage, they happily sit,
For humor's in every leaf and tree.

A porcupine quips with prickly flair,
While fireflies flash with jokes at night.
With glowing smiles, they light the air,
In this playful abode, all feels so right.

So wander where the laughter's thick,
In the woods, where joy's yours to find.
With each step and smile, you'll feel the trick,
For humor in nature is one of a kind!

Shade and Shenanigans

Under the branches, laughter blooms,
Shadows play tricks, banishing glooms.
Squirrels are plotting their nutty surprise,
While whispering jokes that won't win a prize.

A raccoon in sunglasses, struts with flair,
Cracking wise with the skunks in midair.
A tree trunk's a stage for a stand-up show,
As laughter erupts from the leaves far below.

Jokes tossed like acorns, scattered with glee,
Every chuckle a toast to good company.
Nature's funny bone, a comedy scene,
In the shade where mischief reigns evergreen.

So join in the fun, let your giggles resound,
In this leafy haven where joy can be found.
With branches and laughter intertwined and entwined,
A world full of foolishness never maligned.

Greenery's Grinning Secrets

In the thicket, secrets creep and crawl,
Where whispers of giggles echo through all.
The trees wear a grin, leaves rustle and sway,
Sharing silly tales in a leafy ballet.

A wise old owl gives a wink and a nod,
As creatures conspire to play tricks on the sod.
Rabbits in hats with a magician's flair,
Pulling all sorts of surprises from thin air.

Under the canopy, the laughter flows free,
As nature performs its own comical spree.
With each twist and turn, a pun takes its flight,
Beneath the green boughs, the mood feels just right.

So come one, come all, to this joyful delight,
Where shade holds the secrets, and humor takes flight.
In this woodland theatre, where antics align,
The greenery's secrets bring joy that's divine.

Woodland Wordplay Wonders

In a grove full of giggles, puns twirl and sway,
Trees whisper wisecracks on a bright sunny day.
The moss holds the punchlines, soft as a dream,
While laughter erupts like a bubbling stream.

Bees buzz a tune that's both silly and sweet,
As squirrels trade puns while they gather their treat.
Each branch is a stage, every critter takes part,
In the grand woodland circus, with humor and heart.

A fox with a flourish, shows off a new tie,
Cracks up the badgers as they all roll by.
The boughs shake with laughter, a chorus of cheer,
As woodland wordplay is the highlight here.

So join in the fun, let your giggles arise,
With a wink and a chuckle beneath smiling skies.
In this place of pure joy, where laughter's in store,
The wonders of wordplay leave you wanting more.

Boughs of Banter

Among the tall trees, chatter fills the air,
With branches that jive to the whimsy we share.
A chipmunk's witty, with a joke in its pouch,
While rabbits refine their stand-up, that's no slouch.

Boughs sway in rhythm to a pun-filled refrain,
Echoing all the laughter that dances like rain.
A wise old tortoise tells tales that amuse,
As the sun peeks through leaves and the critters enthuse.

Ferns shake with mirth, in their green, gentle way,
As nature comedies unfold in full play.
With a dash of good humor, the forest enjoys,
Unraveling fun in this haven of joys.

So gather your friends, let the chit-chat commence,
Let humor and heart make the wild moments dense.
In this leafy abode, where laughter's the sign,
We celebrate life with all things divine.

Mischievous Musings in the Mist

In the fog, the trees do giggle,
Leaves whisper jokes that make us wiggle.
A squirrel plays tricks with a nut in hand,
Laughter echoes through the forest land.

The shadows dance with playful grace,
While sunlight sneaks to find its place.
A rabbit hops, with a cheeky grin,
In this realm, the fun does begin.

Frogs croak tunes of silly delight,
They croon their songs deep into the night.
And every breeze carries a witty jest,
Nature's humor, at its very best.

So tread lightly where the mischief thrives,
Among the trees, where laughter survives.
With every step, let joy unfurl,
In this wooded realm, a whimsical world.

Jests and Jingles in the Jungle

In the thick of vines, the laughter sways,
Monkeys swing low, brightening our days.
They toss ripe fruit like balls in play,
In the jungle, fun finds its way.

Parrots squawk in colors so bright,
Their squabbles add to the sheer delight.
A snake tells tales with a sly, sly grin,
While the jaguar smirks, let the games begin!

Bamboo clumps tap dance in the breeze,
Jungle creatures playing with ease.
Each rustle and caw brings a crafty pun,
In this playful place, the fun's never done.

As night falls, fireflies blink and tease,
Dancing lights bring laughter like a breeze.
In every corner, there's something to see,
A hidden joke, just waiting to be.

Whimsical Words among the Wilds

In the thicket, tales spin so sweet,
With every twist, new laughter we meet.
A bear hums softly, a curious tune,
As critters gather beneath the moon.

A fox tells stories that stretch and grow,
With puns that dance like the softest glow.
Hopping about, a lively hare,
With words so clever, it's a joyous affair.

Each breeze carries chuckles on high,
As owls hoot secrets from the sky.
The grass sways gently, in a giggling spree,
In this wild place, where we roam free.

So come join the fun, don't miss the chance,
In this magical land, let your heart prance.
Whimsical wonders are all around,
In nature's laughter, joy can be found.

Joyful Echoes in the Underbrush

Among the bushes, giggles abound,
Nature's chorus creates joyous sound.
A raccoon's antics keep us amused,
While the gathering crowd is simply bemused.

Dancing shadows play peek-a-boo,
As the sun sets low, painting skies anew.
A chattering chipmunk shares a sly pun,
In this lively spot, the laughter has won.

With every rustle and playful tease,
Nature's charms bring us to our knees.
Each echo resounds with mirth and zest,
In this underbrush, we feel truly blessed.

So wander these paths, let giggles reign,
In the wilderness where joy is our gain.
Among the undergrowth, laughter takes flight,
In this vibrant realm, everything feels right.

Playful Paths in the Pines

In the shade where squirrels prance,
Life's a game, let's take a chance.
Beneath the boughs, we laugh and tease,
While birds conspire among the leaves.

With every step, a joke unfolds,
Footprints dancing, tales retold.
The pines, they whisper silly dreams,
Where laughter bubbles, or so it seems.

Oh, the knots in tangled roots,
Tickle the soles of laughing boots.
We chase the sun, we dodge the shade,
In every giggle, memories are made.

So stroll with me, let laughter ring,
Among the pines, we'll dance and swing.
On playful paths where spirits fly,
In joyful jest, we'll reach the sky.

Mirth in the Meadow

Out in the field where daisies play,
The sun beams bright, we laugh all day.
With every bloom a giggle grows,
In this patch where silliness flows.

The bees buzz low with cheeky grins,
Tickling flowers where smiles begin.
A butterfly jokes as it flits and flares,
And sunshine chuckles through the air.

Watch out for the grass, it gives a poke,
Yet laughter rises with each little joke.
In the meadow, joy finds its way,
With every chuckle, we sway and sway.

So join the dance, let mirth take flight,
In fields of green, where hearts feel light.
In nature's joke, we find release,
A merry place, where smiles increase.

Chuckle-Sprinkled Sunshine

Through the trees, the sunbeams play,
Sprinkling cheer along the way.
With every glimmer, laughter bursts,
In golden rays, joy freely quirts.

The warmth wraps us in a giggly hug,
As shadows dance, we give a shrug.
With every chuckle, the day grows bright,
In ticklish moments of pure delight.

A breeze comes by with a playful tease,
Whispering jokes in the gentle leaves.
We share a grin as the clouds drift slow,
In the sunny glades where laughter flows.

So let's sip joy like morning's dew,
In gleeful rays, just me and you.
With each bright chuckle, we'll chase the gloom,
In nature's heart, we'll always bloom.

Sassy Shadows of the Pines

In shadows cast by towering trees,
We find the wit of playful breeze.
Each leaf a giggle, each branch a quip,
In every corner, humor's sip.

The pine cones drop with a playful thud,
Rolling laughter right into the mud.
Among the trunks, the sass takes flight,
With whispered jokes that feel just right.

Crouching low, we sneak a peek,
At cheeky creatures who love to sneak.
A secret world of silly plans,
Where even critters join our jests and jans.

So come, dear friend, let's share a smile,
In sassy shadows, let's linger awhile.
Underneath the pines, life's funny scheme,
In laughter's embrace, we find our dream.

Humorous Hikes in the Timberland

Beneath the trees, the squirrels chatter,
A nutty joke, it's all that matters.
Branches sway with laughter's cheer,
Nature's quips, perfectly clear.

A hiker trips, the path is thick,
He'll find his way, it's quite the trick.
Trees stand tall, with winks they say,
Keep your footwork light today.

Amidst the roots, a pun is sown,
Mossy tongues laughing, brightly grown.
What a hoot, the leaves are bright,
Tickling the sun with giggles light.

So pack your snacks and don't delay,
The woodland jokes are on display.
With every step, let laughter rise,
In the forest, joy's the prize.

Cheeky Tales from the Grove

In the grove, the owls confide,
Wisecracks in their nighttime glide.
Frogs with glee, they start to croak,
Each ribbit's just a laughing joke.

A chipmunk holds a tiny mic,
Singing songs of nature's hike.
The acorns roll, with chuckles shared,
"Did you hear? We all are paired!"

Woodpeckers knock in funny time,
Creating rhythms, love their rhyme.
The leaves dance on the playful breeze,
Tickling branches with such ease.

So wander forth with a smile so wide,
Let cheeky tales be your guide.
In every crevice, laughter's found,
In the grove, joy does abound.

Grins in the Gnarled Bark

The gnarled trees wear smiles so sly,
Wooden grins that kiss the sky.
With roots that tickle, spreading cheer,
Nature's jesters, lending ear.

A playful breeze whispers a jest,
Bringing with it a hearty quest.
Leaves tumble down in a happy flurry,
Nature's laughter makes us hurry.

Look closely, see the knots all laugh,
Wooden faces in nature's craft.
Jokes that ring in every park,
Echoing joy in every bark.

So raise a cheer for time spent here,
With every giggle, lose your fear.
In the gnarled bark, let fun embark,
Where the trees hold secrets, lovely and stark.

Captivating Comic Interludes in the Canopy

In the canopy, the laughter soars,
Squirrels' pranks never a bore.
Swinging high with boundless glee,
They share their joy, wild and free.

The birds converse with witty flair,
Chirps that tickle the springtime air.
A sunflower bows, a joke to tell,
Nature's humor casts a spell.

Clouds drift by with a knowing smile,
Winking down, they've traveled a mile.
The sun beams down, a golden wink,
Comedy blooms, a jovial link.

So take a moment, lift your face,
Let lightness bring its warm embrace.
In quiet glades, let laughter bloom,
In nature's theater, find your room.

www.ingramcontent.com/pod-product-compliance
Lightning Source LLC
Chambersburg PA
CBHW071850160426
43209CB00003B/493